~~OLD~~ New WIVES' TALES

by Brenda Nell Davidson

Illustrations by Ed Powers

PRICE/STERN/SLOAN
Publishers, Inc., Los Angeles
1986

Copyright © 1986 by Brenda Nell Davidson
Illustrations Copyright © 1986 by Price/Stern/Sloan Publishers, Inc.
Published by Price/Stern/Sloan Publishers, Inc.
410 North La Cienega Boulevard, Los Angeles, California 90048

Printed in the United States of America. All rights reserved. No part of this publication may be reproduced, stored in a retrieval system, or transmitted, in any form or by any means, electronic, mechanical, photocopying, recording or otherwise, without the prior written permission of the publishers.

ISBN: 0-8431-1494-0

PSS!® is a registered trademark of Price/Stern/Sloan Publishers, Inc.

To Jim and Jason,
Ojai,
and to all the typist clerks in the world.

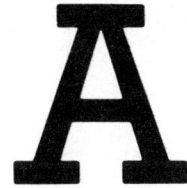

ABOVE-AVERAGE HOUSEWIFE A housewife who always knows where the kids' vaccination records are.

ADOLESCENT Someone who reads Playboy by flashlight.

AEROBIC EXERCISE One more class to feel guilty about not taking.

AFFORDABLE What things are these days instead of cheap.

AGNOSTIC HOUSEWIFE A housewife who's not sure she believes in fabric softener.

ALIMONY

ALIMONY	What the ex-wives of celebrities get. Everyone else gets child support.
ANTISOCIAL HOUSEWIFE	A housewife who refuses to attend Tupperware parties.
ANYTHING TO DO	What people under 14 don't have in July and August.

ASSERTIVENESS TRAINING   What you take to get your husband to say "thank you" when you bring him another cup of coffee.

ATHEIST HOUSEWIFE   A housewife who knows there is no Mr. Clean.

AUGUST   When mothers call their Selective Service Board to see if they ever draft 10-year-olds.

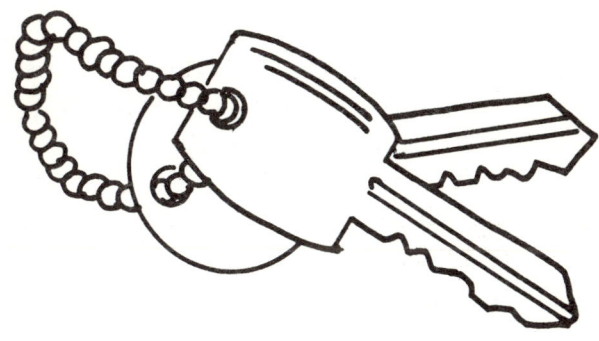

AUTOMOBILE   Just when you've been able to afford a nice new one, a teenager comes up and asks for the keys.

AVERAGE HOUSEWIFE A housewife whose family thinks grey underwear comes that way.

AVOCADO PIT What every housewife spends two years trying to root in a glass above the sink. The toothpicks end up getting root rot.

B

BABY SHOWER   A sacrificial rite in which you give a pastel gift to a pregnant woman. This practice is thought to ward off baby showers in one's own honor.

BABY SITTER   Someone who can't come on Saturday night.

BABY'S CRY   A sound, the pitch of which cannot be heard by the Homo sapiens father, particularly in the middle of the night.

BACK-TO-SCHOOL SHOPPING	What you try to get out of doing with the person going back to school.
BEAUTY PARLOR	Where you go to get the haircut that never looks like the one in the picture.
BELOW-AVERAGE HOUSEWIFE	A housewife whose family thinks grey underwear comes that way, with holes.
BODY WRAP	The length to which some women will go to look good at their 20-year class reunions.
BOIL-IN-BAG VEGETABLES	What you hide under the milk carton in your grocery cart when you see a friend who is a "good" mother coming down the aisle.

BORING HOUSEWIFE A housewife who talks about her job.

BY-THE-BOOK HOUSEWIFE A housewife who waxes in one direction only.

C

CALCULATING HOUSEWIFE — A housewife who's figuring how long she can leave her new slacks in the dryer before they start shrinking.

CALIFORNIA HOUSEWIFE — A housewife who can't decide whether to get a divorce or go to the beach.

CAMPING — What you're doing when you're trying to scrub dried scrambled egg out of a skillet with a leaf.

CAREER-WOMAN HOUSEWIVES — Housewives who do their grocery shopping after work, in heels.

CELLULITE — The cross women bear in exchange for hairlines that don't recede.

CHILD DEVELOMENT — Four-year-old: "Mommy, Daddy, why is the sky blue?"
Fourteen-year-old: "Hey, Mom, hee hee, what's an ovary?"

CHILDLESS COUPLE — People with clean houses who take lots of trips.

CLASS REUNION A meeting where 300 people "hold in" their stomachs for four hours while writing down names and addresses of friends they'll never contact.

CLEAN YOUR ROOM, RIGHT NOW! There is supposedly documented evidence in the Library of Congress that a Richfield, Utah, mother of two didn't have to say this in January, 1957.

CLEVER HOUSEWIFE A housewife who has her husband convinced that soap scum isn't removable.

COLLECTION Everything in your child's room. When asked about those piles of debris, he/she will say, "Oh, that's my collection."

COMMUNICATE

There are three things you can depend on in life: death, taxes and husbands who don't "communicate."

COMPULSIVE HOUSEWIFE

A housewife whose recipe file is in alphabetical order.

CONSCIOUSNESS RAISING

What you're doing when you first realize your husband can butter his own toast. When it dawns on you that he can pick up his own socks, you are a radical feminist.

CONTEMPTIBLE HOUSEWIFE A housewife whose recipe file is in alphabetical order, *by course.*

COWGIRL HOUSEWIFE A housewife whose idea of dressing up is pressing her Levis.

CROISSANT What you can't say right. And if you can, people think you're being pretentious.

D

DATE OF BIRTH   Who wants to know?

DEFIANT HOUSEWIFE   A housewife who knows her mother-in-law is stopping by and doesn't tidy up.

DEFROST   What you do when the freezer door won't close anymore.

DESIGNER CLOTHES — What housewives look at pictures of to find out what they'll be wearing in three years.

DEVIL-MAY-CARE HOUSEWIFE — A housewife who knows her husband's slacks are ready at the cleaners and doesn't pick them up immediately.

DINNER — Even if the world is about to end, someone will figure out a reason why you still have to cook dinner.

DISGUSTING HOUSEWIFE A housewife who irons her castoffs before giving them to Goodwill.

DIVISION OF LABOR The husband cleans the glove compartment and the wife cleans the house.

DIVORCEE DINNER Diet Pepsi, half a box of Triscuits and a paperback novel.

DOMESTIC VIOLENCE Scientists have discovered that 43% of this is committed before 8:00 in the morning over whose turn it is to use the bathroom.

DON'T WAIT UP What teenagers say when they walk out the door at 8 p.m. on Saturday night.

DO YOU KNOW WHAT TIME IT IS? What parents say to teenagers when they walk in at 5 a.m. Sunday morning.

DO YOUR OWN THING

What you should have stopped saying in 1973.

DRIVE-IN MOVIE

Two groups of people go to the drive-in. Everyone under 20 and the people who couldn't get a sitter.

There is a direct correlation between what everyone under 20 is doing and what the people who couldn't get a sitter used to do.

E

EGGPLANT   What you serve in case you haven't heard your child make the throw-up sound lately.

EMPTY NEST SYNDROME   Something that doesn't exist because no one's kids can afford to leave home and get their own apartment anymore.

ENIGMATIC HOUSEWIFE   A housewife who won't tell the secret to her white sauce.

ERRANDS   What you can waste a whole morning figuring out how to postpone.

ERRATIC HOUSEWIFE — A housewife who may cook breakfast, and then again she may not.

ESPRESSO — What you don't like but order anyway to impress other people who don't like it but order it anyway.

EVERYDAY HOUSEWIFE — The only kind there is, unless there's a country where they give you weekends off.

EXCESSIVE HOUSEWIFE   A housewife who irons polyester.

EXERCISE   What you should be doing instead of what you're doing.

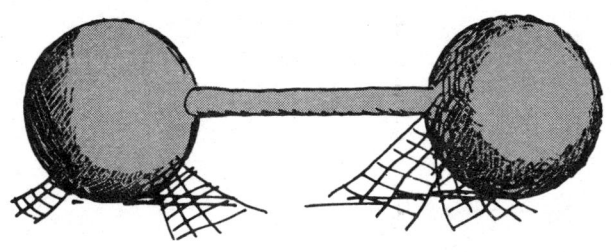

EXHAUSTED, LISTLESS AND DEPRESSED   What American teenagers are when it's time to do chores.

EXHIBITIONIST HOUSEWIFE   A housewife who strips and waxes her floors only when someone is home to watch.

EXISTENTIAL HOUSEWIFE A housewife who says, "I preshrink, therefore I am."

F

FACELIFT Something you used to smirk at the thought of.

FACE THE NATION What you switch to from "Wheel of Fortune" when someone knocks at the door.

FAILURE AT MOTHERHOOD When you're at home with the kids and they miss their baby sitter.

FAMILY VACATION — A contradiction in terms. You can have a family or you can have a vacation, but you can't have both.

FATTY THIGHS — What you buy clothes to try and hide.

FEMINIST HOUSEWIFE — A housewife who reads Ms. Magazine for the recipes.

FIFTH ANNIVERSARY — The year by which you should have gotten rid of the lawn furniture in your living room.

FIRST DAY OF SCHOOL — Comes on the last day you couldn't have taken it anymore.

FLU — Something that strikes teenagers on the day of the math midterm.

FOOD PROCESSOR — Housewife.

FORMAL HOUSEWIFE — A housewife who vacuums in high heels.

FRUGAL HOUSEWIFE — A housewife who re-uses margarine tubs. (A frugal upper-middle-class housewife re-uses butter tubs.)

G

"G"-RATED MOVIE — Means "Guaranteed" not to appeal to teenagers.

GARAGE SALE — Legal minimum requirements for giving a garage sale are: two or more ashtrays from any motel in the continental United States, four lavender plastic flowers, three Readers Digest condensed books and half a set of Melmac dinnerware. Desirable but not mandatory is a cup with a cute saying.

GENERATION GAP What you swore would never happen between you and YOUR child, who then became a teenager.

GOOD IN BED If you have been married more than 10 years, this means you don't steal the covers.

GOOD-LUCK-YOU'LL-NEED-IT HOUSEWIFE A housewife who thinks she can quit her job.

GOOD NIGHT'S SLEEP — What no longer necessarily makes you feel better in the morning.

GOOD WIFE AND MOTHER — A mother who makes original Halloween costumes for her kids.

GROCERY SHOPPING — No matter how much you do this, someone always eats it and you have to do it again. Always shop in grocery stores with Muzak, as they allow you to fantasize that you are in an elevator.

GUILTY MOTHER — A mother whose child has just asked why all those pages in his/her baby book are blank.

GUNG-HO HOUSEWIFE — A housewife who cleans her oven and the family isn't even moving.

H

HAIR DRYER — What, it was discovered in 1972, teenage girls cannot live without.

HAPPY HOUSEWIFE — A housewife who enjoys fixing lunch.

HARD-HEARTED HOUSEWIFE — A housewife who refuses to buy fabric softener.

HARVEST GOLD — Reportedly the color choice of American housewives. Looks like yellow gone bad.

HAUGHTY HOUSEWIFE — A housewife who doesn't do windows.

HELL'S ANGEL HOUSEWIFE — A housewife who kick-starts her vacuum.

HELP OUT (AROUND THE HOUSE) — What most men think they're doing if they remember to put the TV Guide away.

HIPPIE HOUSEWIFE   A housewife who serves Tuna Surprise in a tie-dyed apron.

HOLLYWOOD HOUSEWIFE   A housewife with cleavage.

HOMEWORK — Something teenagers do during commercials.

HOT TUB — Something you sit in for 30 minutes while pretending you're not looking at anyone else's stomach. Said to be a form of relaxation.

HOUSEWIFE WITHOUT CHILDREN — The only kind who's awake for the David Letterman Show.

HOUSEWORK — The natural job of woman, until she can afford to hire someone to do it for her.

HYPERKINETIC CHILD — Anyone under 12 who isn't sick.

I

ICE WATER-IN-HER-VEINS HOUSEWIFE A housewife who can stand there and watch her husband pack his own lunch in the morning.

I'M IN JAIL, MOM The second most-dreaded phone call a parent can receive. The first is news of a nuclear attack.

I'M STILL MARRIED TO YOU, AREN'T I? What husbands say when you ask if they still love you.

IMMACULATE HOUSEWIFE A housewife who dusts her children.

INSUFFERABLE HOUSEWIFE A mother with children the same age as yours who tells you how well they're doing.

INTELLECTUAL HOUSEWIFE — A housewife who washes used plastic forks and asks, "Why?"

IS ANYTHING WRONG? — What husbands ask when you decide not to say anything just to see what he'll say.

IT'S <u>MY</u> HAIR — The first three syllables a fledgling teenager is able to utter. Adolescent equivalent to "mama" and "dada."

J

JADED HOUSEWIFE A housewife who's been around the block too many times to believe the dog broke the vase.

JET-SET HOUSEWIFE A housewife who buys her English muffins in London.

JOB BURNOUT A condition that used to be known as being sick of your job. Mothers and typist clerks are not allowed to have job burnout. You must make over $40,000 a year before you can go away to a weekend seminar on job burnout.

JOGGING SHORTS Wearing apparel that looks better on the rack.

JOLTED HOUSEWIFE   A housewife whose caller has just identified himself as the school principal.

JOVIAL HOUSEWIFE   A housewife who can laugh in the face of the mildewed sheets she forgot in the washer.

JR. HIGH MATH TEACHER   Next to diaper rinsing, the world's most thankless job.

JUBILANT HOUSEWIFE   A housewife whose adolescent has just said:
(a) I need a haircut.
(b) I like my new after-school job.
(c) I hope I make the honor roll this time.
(d) I'm gonna stop hanging around with those guys — they're too rowdy.
(e) May I have some more broccoli?

JUNK FOOD What you disapprove of... except that... well, it's so easy and the kids love it... even though you know it's not good for... but it's so fast...

"JUST A HOUSEWIFE" Something you should never say you are. Store clerks will tell you to have a so-so day. Political parties will ask you for references before you can join. And no one will ever ask what your sign is.

K

KEEPING UP WITH THE JONESES — 80s STYLE

Making sure your satellite dish gets more channels than theirs.

KETCHUP

When adding to an adolescent's food, the item you pour on twice as much as you think a human can stand, then add another half a cup.

KILLJOY HOUSEWIFE

Housewife who matches her husband's socks, giving the rest of us a bad name.

KINDERGARTEN The place which permits you to have two uninterrupted hours to yourself.

KINKY SEX If you have been married over 12 years, kinky sex means leaving the light on.

KITTY LITTER What your two-year-old is probably tasting right now.

KLEPTOMANIAC HOUSEWIFE — The only person in the world who would steal Mop & Glo.

KNOW-IT-ALL HOUSEWIFE — A housewife who always remembers where the Scotch tape is.

L

LAID-BACK HOUSEWIFE   A housewife who thinks water spots on the glasses are proof they've been washed.

LAWSUIT   What everyone is filing over everything these days. An Ohio housewife recently sued her husband because she could have married a doctor.

LAZY HOUSEWIFE   A housewife who buys the peanut butter and jelly already mixed in the jar.

LEARNER'S PERMIT   Something your teenager requests, causing you to renew your Valium prescription.

LEOTARD — Whatever you do, don't wear one of these in front of a mirror.

LETHARGIC HOUSEWIFE — A housewife who thinks spring cleaning is the only time you do it.

LEWD HOUSEWIFE — A housewife who makes anatomically correct gingerbread men.

LIVER SPOTS What scientists had better be working on a cure for.

LIVING WAGE What you hope and pray your teenager will be making someday.

LUCKY HOUSEWIFE A housewife who always picks a grocery cart that goes forward.

M

MADISON AVENUE DREAM HOUSEWIFE

A housewife whose friends come over and look for their reflections in her plates, check her stemware for water spots and sniff the air for signs of household odor.

MARITAL SPAT When he acts rationally and you act just like a woman.

MARRYING UP What once meant marrying a doctor; today it means marrying a microchip repairman.

MARTYR HOUSEWIFE — A housewife who refuses to use Tidy-Bowl or Easy-Off because it would be cheating.

MATHEMATICALLY INCLINED HOUSEWIFE — A housewife who can divide a Reese's Peanut Butter Cup three ways and no one gets the biggest piece.

MEANING OF LIFE — Not something to ponder while scrubbing the bathroom bowl.

MICROWAVE OVEN — Something that takes up all the good counter space.

MIDDLE-AGED — What you became the first time you wondered what this world is coming to.

MIDDLE-AGED REBEL — A housewife who wears shorts in public.

MIDDLE-CLASS REBEL — What you are if you don't keep your yard up.

MID-LIFE CRISIS — What you're having when you decide to start putting makeup on your legs.

MODEL HOUSEWIFE — A housewife who always fixes two green vegetables for dinner.

MOVIE OF THE WEEK — What people who've been married 10 years think of when someone mentions life's greatest pleasure.

MOVING DAY The day that's fun only on TV commercials.

MY KIND OF HOUSEWIFE A housewife whose house is just a little more sloppy than mine.

N

NAG — What the parents of teenagers with hair do.

NAIVE HOUSEWIFE — A housewife who thinks she can stay in bed just because she's sick.

NATURAL CHILDBIRTH — The method used by many women with their first child. Remember, however, that childbirth is the only time in your life that your mother, your doctor and the police all agree that it's perfectly all right for you to use drugs.

NAUSEATED HOUSEWIFE A housewife who'd better start looking at her calendar and counting backwards.

NEGLECTFUL HOUSEWIFE A housewife whose kids think mold comes on Twinkies.

NO-FAULT DIVORCE When you hate each other's guts and no one's to blame.

NO-FRILLS HOUSEWIFE — A housewife who serves her chips without dip.

NON-CONFORMIST HOUSEWIFE — A housewife who can go to a Tupperware party and not buy anything.

NO RESPECT — What Rodney Dangerfield and housewives get.

NOTEWORTHY HOUSEWIFE — A housewife who has never watched "As the World Turns."

O

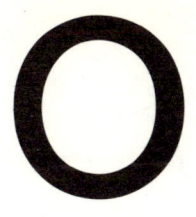

OBSEQUIOUS HOUSEWIFE — A housewife who calls the paperboy "Sir."

OBSOLETE HOUSEWIFE — A housewife who still thinks of Monday as wash day.

OLD-FASHIONED HOUSEWIFE — A housewife who still uses yeast.

105° TEMPERATURE — What your child gets after the doctor's office has closed.

OPPOSITE — What your kids do when you tell them what to do.

OPTIMISTIC HOUSEWIFE   A housewife who thinks her child rearing problems will be over as soon as the kids are grown.

ORNAMENTAL HOUSEWIFE   A housewife with live-in help.

OUTLAW HOUSEWIFE A housewife who operates heavy equipment, such as washing machines and vacuum cleaners, while under the influence of a Librium.

OUT-OF-SHAPE HOUSEWIFE A housewife whose idea of exercise is driving a stick-shift car to the 7-Eleven for ice cream.

OVERACHIEVING HOUSEWIFE A housewife who dusts the top shelf.

OVER-THE-HILL HOUSEWIFE   A housewife who doesn't even care enough to preheat the oven anymore.

OVERTIME HOUSEWIFE   A housewife who knits at the movies.

OVERWEIGHT HOUSEWIFE   Redundant. If you're one, you're the other.

P

PAID HOUSEWORK — All the stray change you find under the sofa cushions.

PANTY HOSE — What you really appreciate if you used to wear garter belts.

PAP TEST — The test you wish you could take as a written.

PART-TIME JOB — What everyone else's kids can find.

pH BALANCED   No one knows what this means, except that every teenage girl in the United States must have it in her shampoo or she'll die.

PIZZA   Gives lie to the "Four Food Group theory" since many teenagers are still alive.

POLYESTER   Something many housewives snubbed until they realized the alternative was ironing.

POSTPARTUM DEPRESSION   Once attributed to hormones in flux, but actually what new mothers get when they realize they can't quit at 5 o'clock.

POWERFUL HOUSEWIFE   A housewife who can separate one grocery cart from another on the first try.

PRACTICAL HOUSEWIFE — A housewife who scrubs mold off the tiles while taking a shower.

PREPPIE HOUSEWIFE — A housewife who mops in Topsiders.

PTA MEETING — Where grown women take sides over chocolate chip vs. oatmeal.

PUNCH-DRUNK HOUSEWIFE — A housewife who's made one too many peanut butter and jelly sandwiches.

Q

QUACK HOUSEWIFE — A housewife who failed Home Ec in high school but got married anyway.

QUAINT HOUSEWIFE — A housewife who wears a girdle.

QUALIFIED HOUSEWIFE — A woman who knows what to do to the fuse box when the power fails on a weekday.

QUARANTINED HOUSEWIFE

A housewife with a two-year-old.

QUICKIE

What married people go to McDonald's for.

QUICK-WITTED HOUSEWIFE

A housewife who can put out a grease fire without letting the bacon burn.

R

"R"-RATED MOVIE   Something that gives teenagers under 17 a chance to practice lying about their age.

RAPT HOUSEWIFE   A housewife whose mind doesn't wander while she's emptying out the lint trap.

RARE HOUSEWIFE   A housewife who still knows how to turn collars.

REFRIGERATOR TEST   What you have passed if you can open your refrigerator right now and not find anything on the back shelf with mold on it.

REMODEL   What you do if you need a surefire excuse for a trial separation.

REPRESSED HOUSEWIFE   A housewife who chops onions so she'll have an excuse to cry.

RETIRED HOUSEWIFE   No such thing. The only retired housewife is a dead housewife.

RING AROUND THE COLLAR   Something an ad agency invented to make wives feel guilty about their husband's dirty necks.

RIPLEY'S BELIEVE-IT-OR-NOT HOUSEWIFE   A housewife who looks good in Spandex.

ROOM MOTHER The one who's supposed to bring the cupcakes. A good room mother brings homemade, a bad room mother brings store-bought. A shrewd room mother brings storebought in a muffin tin.

S

SCHOLARLY HOUSEWIFE — A housewife who reads all the directions on household cleanser cans.

SCIENTIFIC HOUSEWIFE — A housewife who serves Jello in beakers.

SEX OBJECT — What every woman wants to qualify for but not be taken as.

SHAMPOO — What teenage girls must do every 20 minutes, or they'll die.

SLOVENLY HOUSEWIFE — A housewife whose sink has cobwebs.

SMALL TALK

Who can afford a steak these days?...Aren't real estate prices amazing?...Have you tried a store-bought tomato lately?...Don't you think teenagers are worse than ever?...
You're kidding — they seemed so happy together...

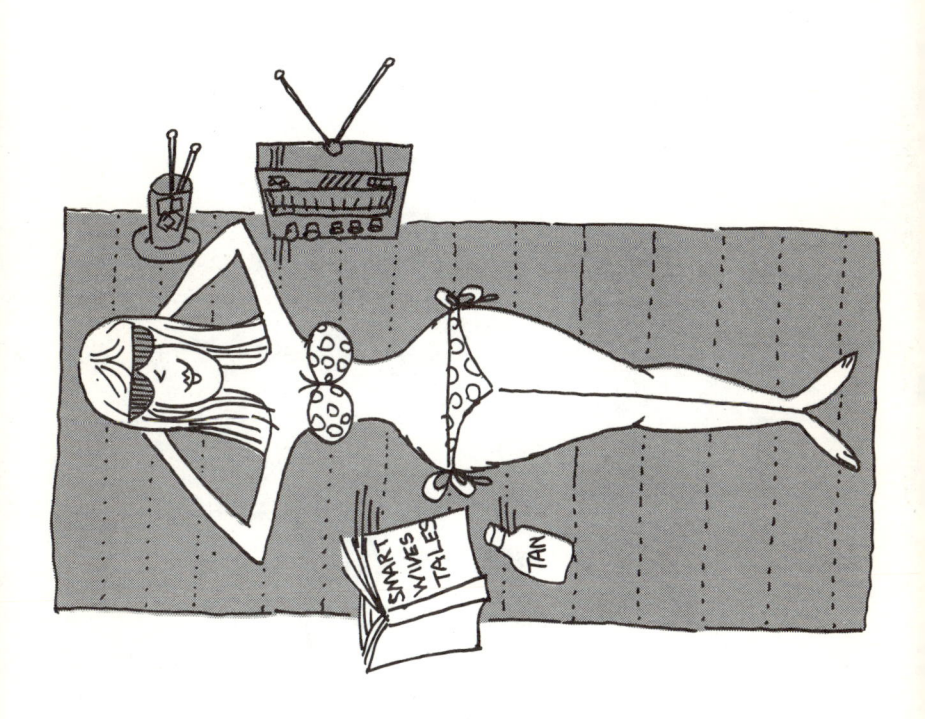

SMART HOUSEWIFE

A housewife who lives in a hotel.

SOCIALITE HOUSEWIFE   A housewife with an uncanny knack for selecting the right greeting card.

SOLVENT   What you have become the first time you can afford frames for your posters.

SORE THROAT   What your child gets the night before the family is to go on vacation.

STATUS — One's social standing. Supreme Court Justice has High Status; Typist Clerk has Low Status. Just-a-housewife has Very Low Status.

STUPEFIED HOUSEWIFE — A housewife whose teenager took out the trash the first time she asked.

SUNTAN — What you work on to hide your varicose veins.

T

TALL HOUSEWIFE   A housewife who wipes off the top of the refrigerator.

THE THRILL IS GONE   When you say you have a headache and he says, "You, too?"

THERMOSTAT — What you turn up when he isn't looking; what he turns down when you're not looking.

THOUGHT PROBLEM — If a divorced father has visiting rights every other Sunday, plus four weekends a year, how many bags of peanuts will he buy at the zoo in July?

THOUGHTFUL AND CONSIDERATE — If your teenager is either or both of these, take his/her temperature.

THRIFTY HOUSEWIFE — A housewife with appendicitis who's saving up for the operation.

TOTAL RECALL — What you have if you are certain you unplugged the iron and turned off the stove before you left.

TOTAL RECALL — What you have if you are certain you unplugged the iron and turned off the stove before you left.

TOXIC WASTE — Whatever is on the back shelf of your refrigerator.

TOY GUN — What many parents start out saying they'll never buy for their children.

TRAPPED HOUSEWIFE — A housewife who has to get a sitter to take a shower.

TUPPERWARE PARTY — A social gathering at which you and everyone else in the room are present because you couldn't say no.

TWO-BATHROOM HOUSE

Two bowls to clean.

TYPIST CLERK

What most working wives in the United States are, but what none of them ever said they wanted to be when they grew up.

U

UNBALANCED HOUSEWIFE A housewife who looks forward to summer because it means more time at home with the kids.

UNDERAGE HOUSEWIFE A housewife with homework.

UNDERWEIGHT HOUSEWIFE No definition. You can't define what doesn't exist.

UNLUCKY HOUSEWIFE Even her plastic plants get aphids.

UNQUALIFIED HOUSEWIFE It doesn't matter. They won't fire you.

UNSCRUPULOUS HOUSEWIFE A housewife who'll substitute margarine in a recipe that calls for butter.

UNSOPHISTICATED HOUSEWIFE A housewife who pronounces the last "r" in Perrier.

UNUSUAL HOUSEWIFE A housewife who's never sold Amway.

UPPER-MIDDLE-CLASS What you are if you grind your own everything, reserve court time and no longer order steak to celebrate.

UPPER-MIDDLE-CLASS FAILURE What you are if you think one brand is just as good as another.

UPPER-MIDDLE-CLASS HOUSEWIFE

A housewife who grinds her own food by choice.

UPSCALE

What you are when you start paying people to hold your cost of living down.

URBANE HOUSEWIFE

A housewife who's already bored with her pasta maker.

V

VACUUM CLEANER BAGS — What you can never remember to get at the store.

VARSITY HOUSEWIFE — A woman who knows her way around a roll of contact paper.

VEGETABLES — If your child requests these, become suspicious. He/She is trying to get on your good side.

VEGETARIAN — What more housewives would be if only there was someone else to do all the chopping.

VELCRO DIAPERS   The greatest invention since the combustible engine.

VERY OLD-FASHIONED HOUSEWIFE   A housewife who does housework in a housedress.

VETERAN HOUSEWIFE   A woman who was cleaning house as far back as World War II.

VIRGIN HOUSEWIFE   A housewife who got a new broom but can't find the directions.

W

WAIST — What 12-year-old girls are going to kill themselves over if they don't get one soon.

WAITRESS — A housewife with tips.

WASTREL HOUSEWIFE — A housewife who doesn't re-use grocery bags.

WAX BUILDUP — Something it would never occur to you to care about if it weren't for commercials.

WEAK SERVE — A problem you have if you are upper-middle-class.

WELL-DRESSED HOUSEWIFE — A housewife whose apron matches the kitchen wallpaper.

WELL-DRESSED TEENAGER — You are well-dressed if your mother sucks in her breath when she sees what you're wearing.

WELL-KNOWN HOUSEWIFE — A housewife who's done something besides housework.

WHAT'S FOR DINNER? — The second most-asked question by adolescents. The first is, "Why can't I?"

WHEN I WAS YOUR AGE... — Lead-in to anecdotes of one's own childhood, made in the presence of unresponsive teenagers.

WHIMSICAL HOUSEWIFE — A housewife who cooks dinner if she's in the mood, and if her nails are dry.

WILL-OF-IRON HOUSEWIFE — A housewife who can resist her children's leftovers.

WOMAN DRIVER — A driver who's willing to stop at a gas station to ask directions.

WOMEN'S RE-ENTRY PROGRAM — What you sign up for when you discover what 10 years of being a good wife and mother means in the job market.

WOMEN'S WORK If someone isn't paying you for doing it, it's women's work.

WORLD'S BEST MOTHER A mother who always has exact change for lunch money.

X

"X"-RATED MOVIE — A movie filled with lurid sex, gutter language and repulsive violence, which your teenager is figuring out how to sneak into.

XMAS SPIRIT — Something wives wish their husbands had more of.

X-RAY VISION HOUSEWIFE   A mother who knows what her child is doing with the modeling clay even though the door is closed.

XYLOPHONE   What you wish your Aunt Helen hadn't given your two-year-old for his birthday.

Y

YARDWORK — What your adolescent will do for anyone else in town for $2 an hour.

YMTTMYSAYMATA? — "You mean to tell me you spent all your money at the arcade?"

YOU'RE NOT GETTING OLDER, YOU'RE GETTING BETTER — World's greatest TV commercial.

YUPPIE HOUSEWIFE   A housewife who's thinking about a cleaning lady.

YUPPIES   People who get away for the weekend and stay at bed and breakfasts.

YUPPIE SNACK   Designer ice cream.

Z

ZANY HOUSEWIFE   A housewife who short-sheets her own children's beds.

ZEALOUS HOUSEWIFE   A housewife who, having driven on a field trip, actually volunteers to drive a second time.

ZUCCHINI   The last word in the dictionary and the last thing your child will eat unless threatened with grounding.

This book is published by

PRICE/STERN/SLOAN
Publishers, Inc., Los Angeles

whose other splendid titles include such literary classics as:

**HOW TO TELL IF
YOUR HUSBAND IS CHEATING $2.95**

IT'S OVER WHEN $2.95

YOU SLEPT <u>WHERE</u> LAST NIGHT? $4.95

FIRST WIFE SECOND WIFE $2.95

and many, many more

The above titles, and many others, can be bought wherever books are sold, or may be ordered directly from the publisher by sending check or money order for the amount listed, plus $1.00 for handling and mailing, to Price/Stern/Sloan's Direct Mail Sales Division at the address below.

For a free list of P/S/S titles, send a self-addressed, stamped envelope to:

PRICE/STERN/SLOAN *Publishers, Inc.*
410 North La Cienega Boulevard, Los Angeles, California 90048

Prices higher in Canada

pss!®